STAY *safe*

your guide to coping with difficult situations

ANITA GANERI

About this book

This book is a guide to staying safe and looking after yourself wherever you are – at school, at home or at play. You never know when accidents might happen. But you can often avoid them by learning how to cope in difficult or dangerous situations. People can be a problem, too, and there is plenty of help and advice in this book about what to do if they try to hurt you. Of course, you may never need to use any of the tips in this book because most of the time you'll be safe. But it's good to know about them, all the same, so that you can be sure to stay safe.

© Anita Ganeri 1994

First published in 1994 by
Health Education Authority
Hamilton House
Mabledon Place
London WC1H 9TX, UK

The right of Anita Ganeri to be identified as the author of this work has been asserted by her in accordance with the Copyright, Designs and Patents Act 1988.

British Library Cataloguing in Publication Data
A CIP catalogue record for this book is available from the British Library

ISBN 1-85448-962-3

Design: Amanda Hawkes
Cover illustration: Tim Kahane
Text illustrations: Tim Kahane and Andrew Warrington
Text photographs: Colin Taylor Productions, British Gas plc (page 31)

Printed in Great Britain

Contents

Accidents will happen

Here are just a few of the places where accidents could happen.

Crossing the road

At home – in the kitchen

At school – in the playground

Near the railway

Near electricity pylons

Going home from school

On a river or canal bank

Cycling on the road

DID YOU KNOW?

About 400 children a year are killed in accidents on the road.

About 750,000 children a year are injured in accidents at home.

That there are lots of things you can do to stop accidents from happening. You can find out about them as you read this book.

HELP IS AT HAND

If there's a fire at home, where would you go for help? If your friend falls into the river and can't swim, what would you do? Where do you turn to if you have a problem and no-one will listen to you? Who can help?

Throughout this book, there are lots of tips for staying safe. There are also lots of children talking about their own experiences and how they coped. You might find you've shared similar experiences. At the back of the book there is a section about how to get help for yourself and for other people. There are names, addresses and telephone numbers of organisations and societies which you can turn to for help.

There may be things in this book that you want to know more about. Find someone to talk to about them – it might be your Mum or Dad, someone else in your family, a teacher, a friend, a friend's parents or one of the organisations given at the end of this book.

Bullying

DEALING WITH PEOPLE

Not everyone you are going to meet is going to be
nice to you. And that includes people who are older
than you, your own age or even younger. A bully is
someone who says or does things to make you
unhappy. There are many different types of bullying.
You might get hit or kicked, called names or a mixture
of both. Do you recognise any of these situations?

*It was awful. It went on for nearly
a year before I changed schools. I just kept
hoping it would stop. The bullies kept on about how
I didn't have a Dad. I do have a Dad but he
doesn't live with us anymore because
my parents are divorced.*

*This girl started picking on me because
I'd got a new school bag. She said I must
have loads of money. She told me to give her
some money, or else.
Then it happened again and again. In the end
I started nicking it from my Mum's purse.
Then my Mum found out ...*

*They kept punching and kicking me
when the teachers weren't looking. I just put
up with it. I thought it was my fault it was
happening. I was scared my Dad would think I was a
wimp. He always told us to fight back if anyone
picked on us. But there were three of them
and only one of me.*

IN THE PLAYGROUND

1. *Look, there's that new girl. She's always by herself.*

2. *I'm not surprised, Who'd want to talk to her?*

3. *I think she looks OK.*

4. *Typical! Come on, let's just ignore her.*

BUT THINK...

Q **Could you really deal with this problem on your own?**

A No, I told my big brother and he told the bullies to leave me alone. They were scared of him because he was bigger than them.

Q **Who could you talk to?**

A I told my Mum in the end. She came to school and told my teacher and my teacher talked to the bullies. It's a lot better now.

Q **Is there anywhere you could go to be safe?**

A Try to stay close to your friends. Find someone to walk to and from school with. Better still, tell someone about the bullying so they can stop it.

Q **Why is the bully acting this way?**

A Most bullies have been bullied or mistreated themselves at some time in their lives. They might be unhappy at home, or not like themselves very much. Some bullies act tough to try to impress people.

Q **Could you ever feel sorry for a bully?**

A I talked to my friend about it and we realised that the bully was always on her own. We started asking her to join in with us. We're all friends now.

Q **What would your advice be to a younger child that this is happening to?**

A They should tell someone as soon as possible. The problem will only get worse. They could go to their teacher or Mum or Dad.

Q **What else can I do?**

A Practise saying "Leave me alone" in a loud, strong voice in front of the mirror. Bullies often pick on people because they think are shy or timid.

Show them that you are not a wimp!

Have you ever bullied anyone?

Racism

There are other forms of bullying, too. Sometimes people pick on others because they are different in some way. They might wear glasses or have red hair or freckles, for example. One of the worst types of bullying is picking on people because of the colour of their skin. This is known as racism.

People go on holiday to get a tan. Then they pick on you if you've got brown skin. I don't understand it.

Some of my friends have white skin and some have brown skin. I never really thought about it before. Then some kids in my class started calling me names ...

I told my Dad and he said the best thing to do was to ignore them. So that's what I did. It hurts me when they call me names so it's hard to ignore them but it's for the best.

WHY DO THEY DO IT?

- They think it's "big" to tease you.

- They feel threatened by you and by the fact you are not exactly the same as them.

- They're trying to win friends by acting tough.

- They're jealous of you in some way.

Treat racism like any other type of bullying (see pages 6–7). Many of the reasons above are the same for any sort of bullying.

BUT THINK...

- Remember – the colour of your skin has nothing to do with being a good or a bad person. Don't let anyone tell you otherwise!

- Be proud of your colour and culture. Then the names and nasty comments won't hurt so much.

- Talk about the problem to your family or friends. That's the best way of finding out that the bully's got a problem, not you.

- It takes all kinds of people to make a world. Without people from different countries and cultures, life would be very dull indeed.

- If someone is teasing you, say "Leave me alone. Go away" in a loud, strong voice, even if you're not feeling very brave at the time. They will often stop.

My best friend's Indian. I go to her house and her Mum cooks us Indian food. It's brilliant. And she comes to my house and my Mum cooks English food.

When you're friends with someone, you don't notice the colour of their skin.

Friends or enemies?

Being part of a gang can be fun. You've a ready-made group of friends to play with and go around with. Or you might have one special friend – your best friend who you go around with and share all your secrets with. (There's more about keeping secrets on pages 20–21.) Friends are very important parts of our lives. But friends can sometimes try to make or force you to do things you don't really want to do. Then they can quickly become enemies.

IN THE SWEET SHOP

A NEW KID IN SCHOOL

When I first joined my gang, they dared me to run across the main road. I did it but I wouldn't do it again. It was really dangerous.

I didn't want to look like a wimp and get thrown out of the gang. I'd never been in a gang before. So I just went along with them. I felt bad about some of the things we did but I still did them.

My best friend's called Hannah. I tell her everything and she tells me everything. It's great. We're always going to be best friends.

③

Oh come on, leave him alone. He can't help it.

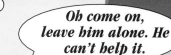

Yeah, leave him alone. Let's go and play football instead.

BUT THINK...

- Having good friends is really great. But having friends who make you do stupid things is just bad news.

- You don't want to look a fool in front of your friends. But if they try to make you do something you don't want to do, say **NO**.

My first best friend went off with someone else. Now I've got another best friend. We go everywhere together and I can tell him everything. It made me realise that my first best friend wasn't a friend at all.

- Yes, you sometimes need to be brave to stand up to your friends. But you might find some of them agreeing with you if you make the first move.

- What would you do if someone dared you to steal money from a shop or from your parents? Or if you saw one of your friends stealing something? Should you say nothing or tell your teacher or parents? Talk to your teacher or parents about the best thing to do.

- Don't try too hard to make friends. Many friendships make themselves.

The dangers of drugs

One of the things your friends (or strangers) may try and make you do is to take drugs of some sort. Drugs are substances which you take into your body and which change the way you are feeling and the way you behave. Some drugs are illegal. This means people can go to prison for having or using them. These are things like cannabis, ecstasy, cocaine, amphetamines and heroin. But other types of drugs, such as cigarettes, alcohol and glue can be bought from shops. It is illegal to buy cigarettes until you are 16 and to buy alcohol until you are 18, but after that no-one can stop you.

Legal or illegal, all these drugs are DANGEROUS. (Alcohol is OK for adults if they don't drink too much.) They are bad for your health and can even kill you. Stay well clear of them. If you are offered drugs, say NO and try to persuade your friends to do the same.

It might be difficult sometimes to say no without feeling stupid but do not let that stop you. Some people find that it helps if they practise saying NO to themselves in a loud and confident voice.

Everyone else used to smoke so I thought I'd try. I just wanted to see what it'd be like.

My friends and I stole some of Mum and Dad's vodka when they were out. We filled the bottles with water so they wouldn't notice. But it made us feel really sick.

Some of the older boys tried to make me sniff glue from a paper bag. I told them that my Mum would kill me if I did and ran away.

If enough people say NO to drugs, people will stop offering them.

If you notice any of your friends acting strangely, it may be because they are taking drugs of some kind. Try to talk to them about it. Show them you care and would like to help them. Here are some signs to look out for:

- Sudden changes of mood
- Secretive behaviour
- Strange smell on breath and clothes
- Slurred speech
- Playing truant from school
- Hanging around with a different crowd of friends, probably older and from outside your school

But, don't jump to conclusions at once. You might have got it wrong. The best thing to do is to talk to someone you trust about it, your teacher or parents. Tell your teacher too if you are being offered drugs at school.

Some people say they take drugs to make them look and feel good. In fact drugs can make you look and feel terrible.

THE FACTS ABOUT SNIFFING, SMOKING AND DRINKING

- When people talk about "glue-sniffing", they mean breathing in the fumes or vapour from substances called solvents. These include some types of glue, nail varnish remover, lighter fuel, paint and aerosol sprays, such as air freshener, furniture polish and hair spray.

- In an average household, there are over 30 substances which can be sniffed.

- Children as young as 7 years old have been known to sniff glue.

- Children have died from heart attacks after sniffing household products such as hairspray, air freshener and furniture polish FOR THE FIRST TIME!

- Alcohol is a very powerful drug. But many people, including your parents probably, drink alcohol as part of their everyday lives. The danger starts when you drink too much or too often.

- Smoking is not illegal if you are over 16. Many kids smoke because they think it looks cool or daring. It isn't! It makes your clothes, your breath and your hair smell and it can seriously damage your health. The poisonous chemicals in cigarette smoke can cause lung cancer, bronchitis and heart attacks. In Britain, smoking kills about one person every five minutes.

- Don't think that it could never happen to you because it could. Be aware and be wise.

- One of the problems with drugs is that you can become addicted to them. This means you can't get by without them. When this happens, all you get are the nasty results of drug taking.

BEHIND THE BIKE SHED

13

Stranger danger

Most people you meet in your life will be perfectly nice to you. But there is no foolproof way of spotting the ones who might want to frighten or even hurt you. The golden stay safe rule is NEVER TALK TO STRANGERS, not even if they know your name or say that your parents have sent them. Another thing to remember is never to go anywhere with anyone who is not part of your family, or someone who your parents have said you can go with.

Even if you know someone a bit, don't go anywhere with them without asking your parents first.

THE FLASHER

The woman who tried to grab me didn't look strange. She just looked normal, like somebody's Mum.

A man stopped his car and called out my name. He told me my Mum had sent him to collect me from school. I nearly believed him. Then my Mum turned up.

Even when I was safe at home, I still thought about the stranger a lot. It made me cry to think about it and I kept having dreams that someone was after me. When I'd told my Mum and the stranger was caught, the bad dreams soon stopped.

THE STRANGER

THINGS THAT MIGHT HELP

If a stranger comes up to you, take no notice, just walk away. Never get in a car with a stranger or even talk to them.

If you are lost or need an adult's help, don't ask a stranger on the street. Go into a shop or ask a policeman or traffic warden.

Try to remember what the stranger looks like, so you can tell someone later. This will help the police to catch the stranger and stop him pestering other kids.

BUT THINK...

● Would you be taken in if a stranger offered you sweets or a present of some sort? Don't be – it could be a trick.

● How do you think a stranger might know your name? Perhaps they saw it on your school books or school bag or heard your friends calling out to you.

● What if the stranger told you that your Mum or Dad was ill and he would drive you home? Don't believe him. Your Mum or Dad wouldn't send a stranger to tell you, even if they really were ill.

● What would you do if you saw a stranger talking to one of your friends? Shout to your friend to come away. Then tell an adult you can trust about what has happened.

Being abused

WHAT IS ABUSE?

You've probably heard people use the word 'abuse' and not known exactly what it means. Abuse is when someone treats someone else in a way that is physically or emotionally harmful, like in the scenes you can see here. There are different sorts of abuse. Someone might touch your private parts when they shouldn't. See page 18 for more about good and bad touches. Or someone might kick or shake or punch you and hurt you that way.

Has anyone ever tried to touch your private parts without you wanting them to? Sometimes, grown ups touch children in a way which hurts them or feels wrong. If this happens, it is not the child's fault, and the adult should not be doing it. But if it does happen to you or if it happens to a friend of yours, here are some tips and advice to help you stop it.

Remember, there is always someone who will listen to you and help you. If the first person you tell won't listen, tell someone else. And keep telling them until they do listen to you. People you might tell include your parents, your teacher, a friend or a friend's parents, or any other grown up you can trust. If you run out of people or don't feel you can talk to someone face to face, call one of the helpline numbers at the back of this book. Then you can talk to an adult who will listen and help.

Don't forget – you have the right to say NO to anything that makes you feel unhappy or hurts. Say it LOUD!

GOOD AND BAD TOUCHES

Good touches

It's OK for your parents to give you a goodnight kiss and hug.
Hugs are good for you.

It's OK to be tickled – just ticklish!

Bad touches

It's not OK for an adult to touch you in a way that hurts you or feels wrong.

It's not OK for an adult to touch the private parts of your body, unless it's your Mum or Dad or a relative giving you a bath or something like that.

Don't feel that you have to suffer on your own.

My Dad started touching me inside my pants. He told me not to tell anyone or else.

Dads aren't allowed to do this. Tell your Dad not to, or tell someone about it.

I told my Mum what my Dad had been doing. She shouted at me to stop lying and gave me a slap.

Your Mum is probably as frightened as you are. Try telling someone else – your teacher, for instance.

My Uncle told me not to tell anyone. He said that even if I told someone, they wouldn't believe my word against his.

That's not true. You must tell someone what your Uncle is doing to you. Turn to pages 20–21 to read more about when to tell.

I keep having nightmares about it. Now I'm scared to go to sleep in case he comes in to my room and it all starts again.

Tell someone about what has happened. That's the only way the problem can be solved and your nightmares can stop.

My Dad tried to trick me by telling me he'd buy me presents and things.

Your Dad knows he's wrong. That's why he thinks he had to buy you a present to make you feel better. Tell him NO.

My Mum held my brother by the arms and shook him so hard he cried. He had great big bruises on his arms after that.

If anyone regularly hurts you by hitting you or shaking you or someone you know, don't keep it to yourself. There are lots of people who can help.

WHAT TO DO

It's difficult, but say NO if any adult tries to touch you and you don't want them to. It's your body, after all.

If you can't talk to your parents, try your teacher or a friend's parents if it's easier.

If you can't think of anyone to talk to, phone one of the telephone helplines on pages 46-47. Someone will always be there to listen to you and to help you.

HOW DO YOU FEEL?

- scared?

- dirty?

- ashamed?

- guilty?

- confused?

- on your own?

WELL, DON'T!
You haven't done anything wrong.

If you find it hard to talk about what has happened to you, try drawing a picture or acting it out with teddies or dolls to show a grown up.

To tell or not to tell?

Have you ever been asked to keep a secret? Perhaps by your best friend, or by your parents? Did you promise not to tell – and did you keep your promise? Keeping secrets is all part of being trusted by other people. And keeping a promise is usually a good thing. But some secrets are better off told, especially if someone is getting hurt or in danger. They might be being bullied or abused in some way. In these cases, you'd be better off telling someone else, like your teacher or parents, so that they can do something to help the person in trouble.

WHEN TO TELL

WHEN NOT TO TELL

② *Oh, nothing. Well, nothing's wrong with me. It's just that I've got a friend and her Dad's been touching her. But don't tell, promise?*

③ *There must be something wrong. Perhaps it's Jenny that's been touched. I'll tell Mum.*

④ *You were right to tell me and I'll do my best to help. Jenny might be cross with you at first but she'll soon see you're a true friend.*

Q My Dad told me not to tell my Mum about her surprise birthday party. But I told her anyway. Did I do the wrong thing?

A Yes! You probably spoilt your Mum's surprise! Some secrets, about nice things like parties or presents, should be kept.

Q My friend was being bullied by some older kids. He made me promise not to tell anyone. But I told the teacher. My friend was really cross with me.

A You did the right thing by telling your teacher. Your friend was obviously miserable and could have got badly hurt. And he'll soon stop being cross with you when he sees that you actually did him a good turn by breaking your promise.

BUT THINK...

- If you think someone is asking you to keep a secret about something bad or dangerous, it's best to tell. Talk to a grown up, like your teacher or parents.

- If someone asks you to keep something secret, and it's a safe secret, you'd be breaking your promise and letting them down if you told.

- Sometimes, whispering about things in a secretive way can make other kids feel uncomfortable. Don't use secrets to make other people feel bad.

- If someone doesn't listen to you or believe you at first, keep on telling them until they do or find someone else to tell. Don't worry about getting into trouble – you could be helping someone out.

Hazards at home

AVOIDING ACCIDENTS

For many children, home is a safe, secure place where they can relax after a hard day at school. But your home is also a place where accidents can happen.

In fact, over half of all the accidents that happen to children happen in their own homes. So, what sort of accidents are they?

The most common are burns and scalds, closely followed by falls and cuts. To stay safe, you need to be careful.

SPOT THE DIFFERENCE

The two pictures below show a safe kitchen and an accident-prone kitchen. Can you spot 10 differences between the two?

DID YOU KNOW?

- In Britain, three-quarters of a million children are injured each year in accidents at home.

- The most common time for accidents to happen is on a Sunday.

> My little brother swallowed a coin he found on the floor. It eventually came out when he went to the toilet, but he could have choked on it.

> I went into the kitchen and poured some orange juice out of the bottle. Only it wasn't orange juice, it was floor cleaner. I went to hospital and had my stomach pumped. It was horrible.

> There was a pan of hot water on the stove. The handle was sticking out and I knocked it off. I got really badly burnt.

> I tripped over a toy on the floor and put my hand through the glass door. I cut my wrist and there was lots of blood. I had to have stitches.

SAFETY FIRST...

- Never touch or swallow anything you're not sure about. Many medicines look like sweets or drinks but they are much more dangerous than that. Even things like Paracetamol tablets, which many people take for headaches, can be dangerous if you take too many of them.

- Don't run around while you're holding a glass or have anything in your mouth. You might trip and hurt yourself.

- Don't play around with plastic bags. Never put one over your head – you could suffocate.

- Watch out for sharp objects such as razorblades in the bathroom. You could easily cut yourself.

Fire safety

More people get burnt and scalded in accidents at home than injured in any other way. Fire and hot water cause more accidents than anything else. You might get scalded if you upset a hot drink or a kettle or saucepan of boiling water.

Fires can start very easily and spread very quickly through a house. If your house has a smoke detector, it will give you extra vital minutes to get out to safety. If you haven't got a smoke detector, talk to your parents about putting one up. Smoke detectors are quite cheap and easy to install. They make a loud beeping noise when they detect smoke. And they could save your life.

I can smell burning. Hold this over your nose and mouth, so you don't breathe the fumes in.

I touched the underneath of the iron. I didn't realise it was still so hot, even though it was switched off. My hand was really burnt. It hurt a lot.

I scalded my foot when I was testing the temperature of the bath water. I screamed.

I knocked a cup of boiling hot coffee over. Some of it only touched my arm slightly but it still burnt me.

> *My Mum told me never to play with matches. They can cause fires.*

> *If you're running a bath, put some cold water in first, then the hot. Then you won't burn yourself.*

> *If you burn yourself, hold the burn under the cold water tap for at least 10 minutes. Then it won't be so painful or swollen. See page 42 for more about how to treat burns and scalds.*

ACTION STATIONS!

If you see a fire:

- Get away from it as quickly as possible. Get everyone out of the house at once.

- Don't waste time or put yourself in more danger by trying to put the fire out.

- If you have to pass through a smoke-filled room, get down on your knees and crawl out. Smoke tends to rise upwards.

- Raise the alarm by telling an adult or dialling 999. Ask the operator for the fire brigade. Tell them your phone number, name and address, where the fire is and what has happened (see pages 40–41 for more about making phone calls).

- If the fire is in your house, don't stop to collect your favourite toys or clothes – just get out. Toys and clothes can be replaced – you can't!

BUT THINK...

- Some nightclothes are made of material which catches fire easily. Check what the label says in your nightie or pyjamas. And don't sit too close to the fire.

- The water in a kettle stays scalding hot for half an hour after the kettle has boiled. So, be careful!

- Remember, remember the 5th of November. Fire isn't just a hazard in the home. Fireworks are fun but never stand too close to them or play with them. You could be risking a very bad burn.

- Ask your teacher if he or she can organise for your class to visit the local fire brigade and talk to some firemen about fire safety.

Electricity

Have a good look around your house or school. How many things can you find which are powered by electricity?

You can't see electricity but you can see what it does. It works the television, computer, washing machine, toaster and the lights around your house.

Electricity comes into your home through sockets in the wall. To reach you, it has made a long journey from the power station where it was made, along a network of wires and cables. It is a very important and useful part of our lives. But electricity can also be very dangerous if you do not use it properly.

This flex is old and frayed. It could be dangerous.

On page 42 you can find what to do if someone gets an electric shock.

Never try to wire a plug yourself. Get an adult to do it for you.

Don't use plugs which are broken or cracked.

Don't pull anything along by its flex.

ELECTRICITY CAN KILL YOU IF YOU MESS ABOUT WITH IT.

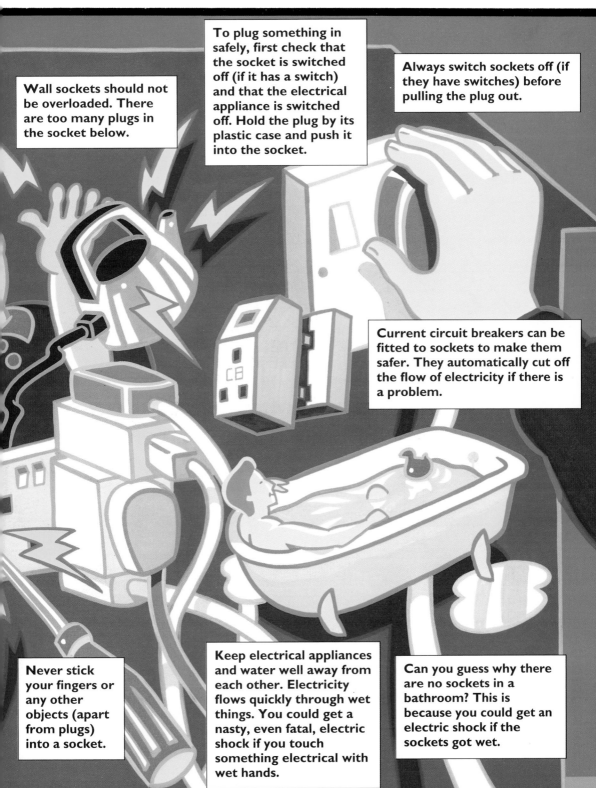

Wall sockets should not be overloaded. There are too many plugs in the socket below.

To plug something in safely, first check that the socket is switched off (if it has a switch) and that the electrical appliance is switched off. Hold the plug by its plastic case and push it into the socket.

Always switch sockets off (if they have switches) before pulling the plug out.

Current circuit breakers can be fitted to sockets to make them safer. They automatically cut off the flow of electricity if there is a problem.

Never stick your fingers or any other objects (apart from plugs) into a socket.

Keep electrical appliances and water well away from each other. Electricity flows quickly through wet things. You could get a nasty, even fatal, electric shock if you touch something electrical with wet hands.

Can you guess why there are no sockets in a bathroom? This is because you could get an electric shock if the sockets got wet.

Gas alert

Gas is another important source of power which we use to cook our food and heat our homes. But, like electricity, it can be very dangerous if we don't treat it properly. Do you have a gas cooker or gas fire in your home? You can't see gas – it has no natural colour, taste or smell. But a strong, artificial smell is added to gas before it reaches your home. This is so that, if there is a gas leak, you can smell it and get out of the way.

IF YOU SMELL GAS...

Tell an adult.

Open the windows and doors to let the gas out.

Get an adult to help and turn off the gas supply at the gas meter.

Don't light a match – you may cause an explosion. And, don't let anyone light up a cigarette.

Don't switch the lights on or off.

Check that the gas cooker and gas fire haven't been left on accidentally.

Phone the gas people and report the leak. You'll find the number in the phone book, under GAS.

Have you ever seen a gas sniffer van? They patrol the streets sniffing out gas leaks.

THE STORY OF GAS

Gas formed millions of years ago from the bodies of billions of tiny sea animals and plants.

Today, it is found deep in the ground. To reach the gas, a well has to be drilled into the rock. Then the gas is pumped out and carried along pipelines. It is treated and measured in a gas terminal, then it travels along a network of smaller pipes to factories, schools and homes.

Play safe

There's nothing better than playing outside with your friends on a warm, sunny day. And normally, you go home afterwards, safe and sound. As usual, however, accidents can happen and some places are much safer to play in than others. Here are some dos and don'ts to keep you safe while you're having fun.

Never fly kites or model aircraft near electricity pylons or cables. You could be badly hurt or even killed by an electric shock.

Be careful in the playground. It's easy to graze your knee, get a bad bruise or even break an arm or leg.

Don't fish near electricity pylons. Your line might get tangled up in the cables when you cast it.

If there's a wasp or bee about, don't flap your hands at it. You'll irritate it and make it more likely to sting you. Keep still and it will soon go away.

If you're wearing a long scarf, take it off before you go on the swings or a roundabout. It might get caught. Watch out for your fingers, too!

DID YOU KNOW?

- The main playground injuries are cuts, grazes, bruises and broken bones.

- In Britain, doctors and hospitals treat about 100,000 playground injuries each year.

Don't tease stray dogs. They might bite you if you scare them or make them angry. If a fierce dog comes near, stand still and don't stare at it. It will soon lose interest in you and go away.

Don't walk behind someone on a swing. You might get hit.

Keep well away from building sites. There are all sorts of accidents waiting to happen on them.

Don't ride roller skates or skateboards on roads. Cars might find you difficult to see. Wear helmets, knee and elbow pads to soften your landing if you fall over.

DON'T GET TOO ALARMED! STAY SAFE AND HAVE FUN!

THE RAILWAY CODE

Railway embankments and station platforms can be very dangerous places indeed. Here are a few tips to keep you safe:

● Never, ever go on to a railway track. You can't always hear high-speed trains approaching until it is too late. Many lines are electrified so you also risk being electrocuted.

● If you're waiting for a train, don't stand too close to the edge of the platform. There is usually a line for you to stand behind.

● Never ride your bike or skateboard on a station platform. It is dangerous and against the law.

● If the barrier is down at a railway crossing, don't try to run across the track. The train may only be a second or two away.

Road safety

You need to keep your wits about you when you are out on the roads. Each year, in Britain, about 400 children are killed on the roads and hundreds more are seriously injured. Most of them are pedestrians who are hit by cars, either because the cars didn't notice them or because they didn't notice the cars. Don't let this happen to you or your friends. A knowledge of road safety could save your life.

> *I heard the ice-cream van and ran out into the road. Next thing I knew, I was in hospital with a broken leg.*

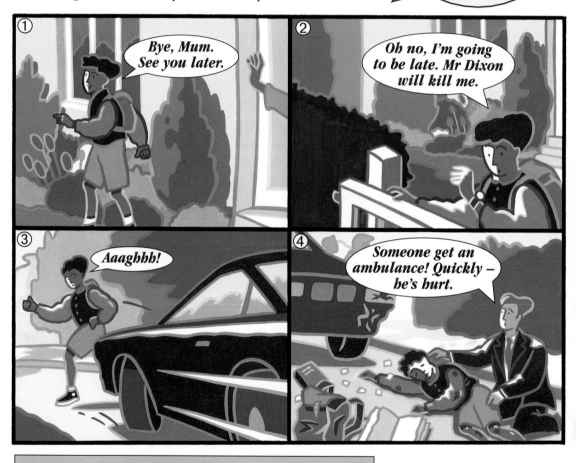

DID YOU KNOW?

- In total, an average of 100 people are killed each week on the roads in Britain.
- Children aged between 8 and 11 are most at risk of being run over.
- Most road accidents happen in daylight.

> *My brother and I were playing football and my brother kicked the ball into the road. He ran to get it. Then there was a terrible crash and I heard screaming.*

> *My friend was hit by a car. The driver said he didn't see her in the dark.*

BUT THINK...

- Is there a traffic club or road safety club at your school? If not, how about starting one up?

- If you're not very tall, car drivers might have a hard job seeing you in a busy, built-up area. Make sure drivers can see you.

- Judging a car's speed and distance away is a life-saving skill you need to learn. Don't take any chances – always give yourself more time than you think you might need, just to be on the safe side.

- How good a pedestrian are you? Do you always look out for hazards when you cross the road, such as cars overtaking, the traffic lights changing suddenly, cars failing to stop at red lights and **STOP** signs?

- Are your friends good pedestrians? How can you help them become safer road users?

> *My teacher helped me find a route to school with lots of safe places to cross the road.*

> *When we're in the car, my Dad tells me what the road signs mean. That's helpful when I'm crossing the road on my own.*

> *At night, you should wear clothes which show up in the dark. Then car drivers can see you easily.*

THE GREEN CROSS CODE

1 Find a safe place to cross the road. Then stop.

2 Stand on the pavement, not too close to the kerb.

3 Look to the right and left for any traffic. And listen out for traffic approaching.

4 If the road is clear, walk straight across.

5 If there is traffic coming, stay where you are. Let the traffic go past, then look right and left again.

6 Carry on looking and listening for traffic as you are crossing the road.

Safe cycling

The rules of the road apply whether you are walking, a passenger in a car or cycling. Most cycling accidents happen when a car hits a cyclist. And the most serious injuries that cyclists suffer are to their heads. This is why cycle helmets are so important – they really do save lives. Learning how to ride your bike properly and safely is a skill which needs patience and practice. But it'll be worth it in the end!

Learn the rules of the road and how to ride your bike properly. Ask at school to see if you can do the Cycling Proficiency Scheme. This will teach you safe cycling and you'll earn a badge and a certificate.

Wear a cycle helmet – you'd be silly not to. Make sure your helmet is the right size and of the right standard. You can ask for advice in your local bike shop.

Wear clothes that will get you seen, for example, reflective clothing at night. You can get reflective vests and armbands, and reflective stickers to stick on your cycle. You must use front and back lights, and a red back reflector at night. It's against the law not to.

Make sure your lights are clean and in good repair. The same goes for your cycle. Check that your tyres are blown up and that your brakes are working. Check that your handlebars and chain are tight enough and that your bell can be heard.

It's illegal, and dangerous to cycle on pavements. Many towns have special cycle ways. Use them wherever you can.

Your bike should be the right size – for you!

Many injuries happen when riders fall off their bikes, attempting stunts and tricks. Be careful!

Ride in single file on narrow or busy roads. Keep your eyes on the road and stay alert at all times. Don't rush out between cars without looking all around first.

Don't overload your bike, either with people or baggage. Keep your hands free for making signals, not holding onto luggage.

DID YOU KNOW?

- Three-quarters of all cycling injuries happen to children aged between 10 and 14.

- More than a thousand children are injured in cycling accidents each year in Britain.

Water safety

Do you ever go fishing or walking by the river or canal? Do you like swimming, canoeing or sailing when you're on holiday? Playing in or near water can be perfectly safe, as long as you are careful. But it is possible to drown in just a few centimetres of water, so it is vital that you have some knowledge of water safety. And, most importantly, can you swim?

I swam too far out to sea. Then I got tired and couldn't swim back. Luckily someone saw me and came and rescued me.

The pond in the field at the back of our house froze in the winter. I was walking on the ice. It was fun. Then I heard a cracking sound and I fell in. The water was really cold. My Dad managed to get me out.

① WARNING! THIS CANAL IS DANGEROUS.

② Help! Help! I can't swim!

③ Here, hold on to this and try to float.

④

> *We go to the swimming pool every week. We feel really safe because there's always a lifeguard there.*

> *Come quickly. My friend's fallen in the canal. And he can't swim.*

For every person who dies from drowning, there are two who are saved by someone else acting quickly and knowing how to resuscitate them. You can learn about resuscitation on life-saving courses.

WATER SAFETY TIPS

- Learn to swim! And to life save.
- Never play in or near water on your own. It's possible to drown even in a garden pond or paddling pool.

- Look out for notices. If there is a sign telling you to keep out of the water, then Keep Out!
- Don't swim in fast-flowing rivers. They often have strong currents which might sweep you away.

- Never dive into swimming pools without finding out how deep the pool is first. You could hit your head and injure yourself very badly.
- Avoid dirty water – it can spread diseases and infections.

- If you do fall in, try not to panic. Try to stay upright and to tread water. Call out or raise an arm to attract attention.

- If you're out in a canoe or boat, wear a buoyancy aid or life jacket. Then you'll float if you fall in.

Help is at hand

DIALLING 999

If there is an emergency, go to the nearest phone and phone the emergency services – the fire, police or ambulance services. These calls are free, so you do not need any coins even if you are using a payphone. Here's what you should do:

Pick up the receiver. Depending on the type of phone it is, dial or press the buttons for the numbers 999.

The operator will ask you your phone number and which service you need.

ACCIDENTS AND EMERGENCIES

How do you think you'd cope in an emergency, such as a fire or a road accident? There are lots of things you could do to help.

First, though, you need to keep calm. Take a few deep breaths if you feel panicky.

The next thing to do is to tell a grown-up what has happened, if there is someone about. If there isn't, you may need to give first aid and phone for help. You can learn about first aid on pages 42-43. On these two pages, you can find out about making phone calls. But remember, help out if you can but not if it will harm you too.

Tell the operator your number and ask for the fire brigade, police or ambulance.

If you say ambulance, you will be put through to the ambulance services and so on.

Tell them your phone number again, your name and address and what the emergency is.

REMEMBER...

- Only make an emergency call if there is an emergency. Someone else may really need the ambulance.

- Practise making emergency calls with a friend. One of you can play the part of the operator and the other of the caller.

- Stay where you say you are until the ambulance arrives. Otherwise they may waste valuable time trying to find out where they are needed.

TELEPHONE SAFETY TIPS

- Normally, when you make a call from a payphone you need to pick up the receiver, put a coin in the slot (most phones take 10p, 20p, 50p and £1 coins), then dial or press the number. But, in an emergency, you can dial 100 free and get through to the operator who will help you. There are some useful helpline numbers on pages 46-47.

- If you are on your own at home and the phone rings, don't say your name and phone number even if you think you recognise the caller's voice. Don't tell the caller that you are on your own. Make an excuse as to why your parents can't answer the phone, for example, your Mum's having a lie down or your Dad's in the shower. Ask the caller to give you their number so your Mum and Dad can call them back. If the caller is a hoax, he or she will probably ring off.

- There are people who use the telephone for a thrill. They phone people up and breathe hard or say rude things down the phone. If this happens to you and you're on your own, never answer back. Simply hang up the phone. If it happens again, take the phone off the hook or call a friend or relative. Always tell your parents what has happened when they get home.

First aid

In an emergency, you may have to wait a short while for the ambulance or fire engine to arrive. If someone has been hurt or injured, they may need immediate help to stop their injuries getting worse. This is when it is useful to know some basic first aid. Try to remain cool and calm. If you have any doubts about what to do, wait for the doctor or ambulance or find a grown up.

BURNS AND SCALDS

- DO hold the burnt or scalded area under cold, running water for at least 10 minutes.

- DO cover the burn with a clean, dry cloth such as a tea cloth or handkerchief.

- DON'T put cream or ointment on a burn.

- DON'T prick blisters. The wound may get infected.

- If someone's clothes have caught fire, DO make them roll on the ground or cover them in a rug or blanket to smother the flames.

CHOKING

- DON'T try to get the object out of the person's mouth.

- DO lay the person face down across your lap (if you can) and give them two or three hard thumps between their shoulder blades.

- DO call for a doctor or an ambulance.

ELECTRIC SHOCK

- DO turn the power off before touching the person.

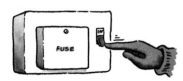

- If you can't turn the power off, DO push the person away from the power with a wooden object such as a chair or broom handle.

CUTS AND GRAZES

If the cut is bleeding a lot, DO press on it firmly with a clean cloth for 10–15 minutes until the bleeding stops.

- DO raise the cut part up, if you can. This will help to stop the bleeding.

- DO cover the wound with a clean, dry dressing (a clean, folded up hanky will do). If blood starts to seep through, DON'T remove the dressing. Put another dressing on top of it.

- DON'T try to remove anything that is stuck in the cut, for example, a piece of glass or a nail.

BROKEN BONES

- DON'T move the person unless it is absolutely necessary

- If you have to move the person, DO support the broken limb by putting one hand above it and one hand below it.

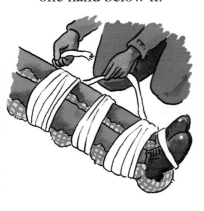

- If you can, DO strap the broken limb to another part of the body (for example, a broken leg to the unbroken leg). But DON'T try this if it causes the person too much pain.

- DON'T bend the broken limb.

POISONING

- If the person has swallowed bleach or another household chemical, DO give them milk or water to drink.

- DON'T give the person salt or salty water to drink.

- If possible, DO keep the container they have drunk from to give to the doctor. If the doctor can identify what the person drank, he or she can help them more quickly.

DROWNING

- If you see someone in trouble in the water, DO throw them something which will float and which they can hold on to. This might be a beach ball, a rubber ring or a branch.

- DO call for help.

- DON'T jump in after the person unless you can swim well.

- DO take a life-saving course – you might be able to save someone's life. You will be taught how to do mouth-to-mouth resuscitation which can save a person's life.

You and your rights

Just as you have the right to have food to eat, to sleep at night and to play with your friends, so you have the right to stay safe. People, such as bullies or flashers, who try to hurt children, are taking away those rights. But there is now a special law, called the Children Act, which sets out rules and guidelines to protect your rights and keep you safe. The rules and guidelines are for parents, courts and local authorities to follow.

THE MAIN POINTS

- Previous acts stressed the rights of parents over their children. The Children Act stresses parents' responsibilites towards their children.

- The aim of the Children Act is to protect the rights of children.

- The welfare and well-being of children is the most important thing.

- The children's wishes and feelings must be taken into account, wherever possible.

- For the first time, the Children Act says that a child's race, culture and religion should be taken into account in any decisions made about their lives.

- Children now have the right to apply for certain orders, for example, "No Contact" orders. These mean that the children do not want contact with their parents.

- Any action that is taken by the courts or local authorities should improve the care of children.

- Services should be provided to stop abuse of children and to help disabled children lead normal lives.

- Children will have access to counselling and advice.

- The Children Act is designed to make family break-up less traumatic for children and parents.

STANDING UP FOR YOURSELF

- SAY NO (however hard it may be)

- GET AWAY TO A SAFE PLACE AS FAST AS YOU CAN

- TELL AN ADULT YOU TRUST

- KEEP ON TELLING UNTIL SOMEONE BELIEVES YOU

Not everyone has someone to talk to. On pages 46-47 there are lots of phone numbers and addresses of places you can turn to. Don't be scared to contact them for help.

Who can help?

You can write to or phone the societies and organisations listed here for help and information about staying safe.

Some of the helpline numbers given below are free and open all day and night. There will always be someone there to listen to you if you have a problem.

ACCIDENT PREVENTION

Child Accident Prevention Trust
4th floor
Clerks Court
18–20 Farringdon Lane
London EC1R 3AU

0171-608-3828

Royal Society for the Prevention of Accidents
Cannon House
The Priory
Queensway
Birmingham B4 6BS

0121-200-2461

National Playing Fields Association
25 Ovington Square
London SW3 1LQ

0171-584-6445

The Royal Life Saving Society UK
Mountbatten House
Studley
Warwickshire B80 7NN

0152785 3943

Kidscape
152 Buckingham Palace Road
London SW1W 9TR

0171-730-3300

The Electricity Association
Education Department
30 Millbank
London SW1P 4RD

0171-344-5700

British Gas PLC
Rivermill House
152 Grosvenor Road
London SW1V 3JL

0171-821-1444

Britax (Travel Safety)
1 Churchill Way West
Andover
Hampshire SP10 3UW

01264-333343

Health Education Authority
Hamilton House
Mabledon Place
London WC1H 9TX

0171-383-3833

HELPLINES

ChildLine
0800 11 11 (free; 24-hour)

NSPCC Child Protection Helpline
0800 800 500 (free; 24-hour)

The Samaritans
see your local telephone directory (free; 24-hour)

Drugs
dial 100 and ask for Freefone Drug Problems

CHILD SAFETY

National Children's Bureau
8 Wakley Street
London EC1V 7QE

0171-278-9441

National Society for the Prevention of Cruelty to Children (NSPCC)
42 Curtain Road
London EC2A 3NH

0171-825-2500

NCH Action for Children
85 Highbury Park
London N5 1UD

0171-825-2500

Re-Solv (The Society for the Prevention of Solvent Abuse)
30A High Street
Stone
Staffordshire ST15 8AW

01785-817885

Al-Anon
61 Great Dover Street
London SE1 4YF

0171-403-0888

ASH (Action on Smoking and Health)
109 Gloucester Place
London W1H 3PH

0171-935-3519

HELP FOR PARENTS

Parentline
01268-757077

Parents Anonymous
0171-263-8918

Index